Different Spikes & Spines of Animals

by Grace Hansen

Abdo Kids Jumbo is an Imprint of Abdo Kids
abdobooks.com

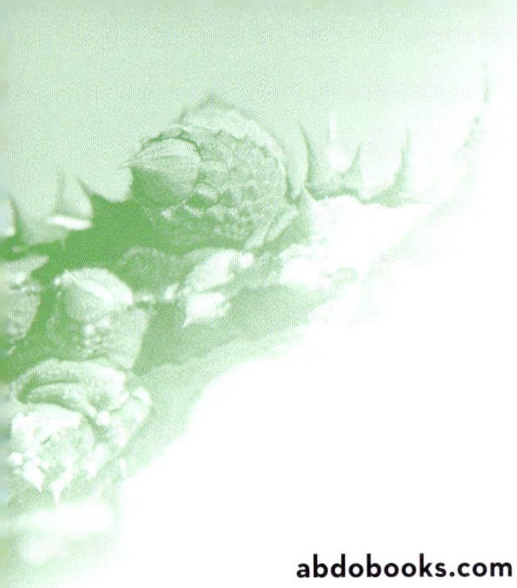

abdobooks.com

Published by Abdo Kids, a division of ABDO, P.O. Box 398166, Minneapolis, Minnesota 55439.

Printed in the United States of America, North Mankato, Minnesota.

052023

092023

THIS BOOK CONTAINS RECYCLED MATERIALS

Photo Credits: Alamy, BluePlanetArchive.com, Getty Images, Shutterstock

Production Contributors: Teddy Borth, Jennie Forsberg, Grace Hansen
Design Contributors: Candice Keimig, Pakou Moua

Library of Congress Control Number: 2022946795

Publisher's Cataloging-in-Publication Data

Names: Hansen, Grace, author.

Title: Different spikes & spines of animals / by Grace Hansen

Description: Minneapolis, Minnesota : Abdo Kids, 2024 | Series: Amazing animal features | Includes online resources and index.

Identifiers: ISBN 9781098266271 (lib. bdg.) | ISBN 9781098266974 (ebook) | ISBN 9781098267322 (Read-to-me ebook)

Subjects: LCSH: Animals--Juvenile literature. | Body composition--Juvenile literature. | Spikes--Juvenile literature. | Zoology--Juvenile literature.

Classification: DDC 591.1--dc23

Table of Contents

Animals with Spikes and Spines

Some animals have spikes and spines. These pointed body parts help protect them from hungry **predators**.

Rodents

Porcupines are rodents with stiff hairs called quills. Each porcupine has about 30,000 of them! If a **predator** touches the quills, the quills stick into the animal's body. It is painful!

Mammals

Hedgehogs are nearly covered in prickly spines. When they feel scared, they roll into a tight ball. All that **predators** can see and touch are spikes!

Echidnas live throughout Australia, Tasmania, and New Guinea. They have beige and black spines. Their spines help them hide in **brush**. If a **predator** finds them, echidnas roll into a ball.

Reptiles

Thorny devils are lizards. They live in Australia. They are covered in pointy spines. Their sharp spines are enough to keep most **predators** away.

Thorny devils have small **grooves** between their spines. Water from **dew** and rain collects there. The water flows toward the lizard's mouth so it can drink.

Spiders

Spiny orb-weavers have bright colors and oddly shaped bodies. The colors warn birds to stay away! Their shapes and spines make them very hard to eat.

Fish

Porcupine fish are covered in spiny scales. If they feel threatened, they make themselves bigger by puffing up their bodies. When they puff up, their spines stick out.

Lionfish are known for their **venomous** fin spines. If they feel scared, they stiffen their fins and attack. Their needle-sharp spines can hurt animals. The venom can cause pain and death.

More Animal Spikes and Spines!

Armadillo Lizard

Sea Urchin

Orange-Striped Oakworm

Spiny Flower Mantis

Spiny Leaf Insect

Crown of Thorns Starfish

Glossary

brush – a thick group of small trees, shrubs, or bushes growing together or land covered by thick growth of plants or trees.

dew – little drops of water that collect at night on cool surfaces.

groove – a long narrow cut or dent in a surface.

predator – an animal that hunts other animals for food.

venomous – producing a fluid, called venom, that is poisonous to humans and animals.

Index